# Exercise!

# SPEED

## Get Quicker!

Ellen Labrecque

**www.raintreepublishers.co.uk**
Visit our website to find out more information about Raintree books.

**To order:**
☎ Phone 0845 6044371
📄 Fax +44 (0) 1865 312263
📧 Email myorders@raintreepublishers.co.uk

Customers from outside the UK please telephone +44 1865 312262

Raintree is an imprint of Capstone Global Library Limited, a company incorporated in England and Wales having its registered office at 7 Pilgrim Street, London, EC4V 6LB – Registered company number: 6695582

Text © Capstone Global Library Limited 2013
First published in hardback in 2013
The moral rights of the proprietor have been asserted.

Edited by Rebecca Rissman, Daniel Nunn, and Sian Smith
Designed by Steve Mead
Picture research by Ruth Blair
Production by Victoria Fitzgerald
Originated by Capstone Global Library Ltd
Printed and bound in China by Leo Paper Products Ltd

ISBN 978 1 406 24204 1 (hardback)
16 15 14 13 12
10 9 8 7 6 5 4 3 2 1

**British Library Cataloguing in Publication Data**
Labrecque, Ellen.
  Speed. -- (Exercise!)1. Speed--Juvenile literature. 2.
Physical fitness--Juvenile literature. I. Title II. Series
  612.7'6-dc22

**Acknowledgements**
We would like to thank the following for permission to reproduce photographs: Alamy pp. 11 (© Jeff Greenberg), 22 (© Radius Images); © Capstone Publishers pp.13, 15, 17, 21 (Karon Dubke); Corbis pp. 8 (© MM Productions), 24 (© Gary Houlder), 25 (© Anderson Ross/Blend Images); Getty Images p. 9 (JOE KLAMAR/AFP); Shutterstock pp.5 (© wavebreakmedia ltd), 6 (© Morgan Lane Photography), 7 (© Cameron Cross), 10 (© AISPIX), 18 (© JJ pixs), 19 (© Konstantin Sutyagin), 23 (© aceshot1) 27 (© holbox), 27 (© Monkey Business Images), 28 (© Fotokostic), 29 (© sportgraphic).

Cover photograph of Marko Devic of Ukraine (R) and Shavkat Mullajanov of Uzbekistan during a game in 2011 in Kyiv, Ukraine reproduced with permission of Shutterstock (© katatonia82).

We would like to thank Victoria Gray for her invaluable help in the preparation of this book.

Every effort has been made to contact copyright holders of material reproduced in this book. Any omissions will be rectified in subsequent printings if notice is given to the publisher.

# Contents

Some words are shown in bold, **like this**. You can find out what they mean by looking in the glossary.

# Let's get fit!

Exercise does each part of your body good. That's why it's time to make fitness a part of your daily routine, just like brushing your teeth, or eating healthy food. Exercise keeps you fit, it makes you feel happier, and it can even help your brain to work better!

So let's get moving . . . that is what your body is built to do!

**BY THE NUMBERS**
The average person takes about 3½ million steps every year.

It's time to get up and get moving!

# What is speed?

There are five different parts of fitness. They are **stamina**, flexibility, **coordination**, strength, and speed. Do you want to run extremely fast? Then you need to develop the right kind of muscles. These are the muscles that make the short bursts of speed needed to race down a running track, or your street.

Racing each other can be fun.

There are many exercises you can do to train the muscles that help you move quickly.

# Start slow

When you train for speed, it is very important to **warm up** your muscles first. If you instantly move from sitting around to running as fast as you can, you will **strain** a muscle.

There are many different stretches you can do to help your body to warm up.

It is especially important to stretch your legs. Once your muscles feel warm, jog slowly before you run fast. This will help your muscles to warm up even more.

## BY THE NUMBERS

The cheetah is the fastest land animal. It can run at 112 kilometres per hour (70 miles per hour). Usain Bolt, the champion sprinter, can run up to 45 kilometres per hour (28 miles per hour).

# Running on a full tank

Exercising, especially running, takes a lot of energy. You should eat about two hours before you plan to run. Make sure you take breaks to drink.

Take a bottle of water with you when you exercise.

It is important to stay **hydrated** while you train. The harder you work, the more water you lose through **sweating**. You need to replace the water you lose, or you will run out of energy.

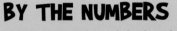

**BY THE NUMBERS**
Children should drink six to eight glasses of water per day.

When you run you feel your body getting hotter and you sweat more.

# Running right

One of the best ways to get faster is by learning to run correctly. These tips will help you to look like a professional:

1. Stand tall when you run. Keep your hips and shoulders in line.

2. Your feet should point straight forward. Don't let them roll out to the sides.

3. Hold your arms at a right angle (like the corner of a square). Keep them close to your body and move them smoothly back and forth. They should not cross your body, but stay in a straight line.

# Frankenstein walk

**Exaggerating** parts of your running moves will help you to improve your running. It will also make you faster.

One of the best exercises is walking like a monster. (It's fun too!) Stick your hands out straight in front of you. Keep your knees straight and raise one leg at a time as high as possible towards your hands.

## MINI CHALLENGE BOX

Walk like a monster for 50 steps, then turn around and do the same thing coming back. (Feel free to growl or roar!)

# Bottom kick

Another way to **exaggerate** your running motion is to do a bottom kick! Lean forwards slightly, so that you are ready to run. With your arms bent, run so that your feet kick your bottom.

The steps should be really quick, and you should lightly touch your bottom with your foot each time.

**MINI CHALLENGE BOX**
Do this exercise for 50 steps, then turn around and repeat.

# Find a hill

Running down a hill is fun, and also teaches you to be faster! Try running down a hill as fast as you can. Make sure the bottom of the hill is safe and grassy.

Run at a speed that feels safe to you.

Your body will get used to moving more quickly and to taking longer **strides**.

**MINI CHALLENGE BOX**
Run down the hill five times in a row. Jog back up the hill or walk in between each run.

# Basketball slides

Sideways skips while bending the knees are called basketball slides. They really teach you to get your feet moving!

Slide with your right leg, then bring your left leg to meet the right. Keep repeating and move as quickly as you can. Your arms should be bent in the running position.

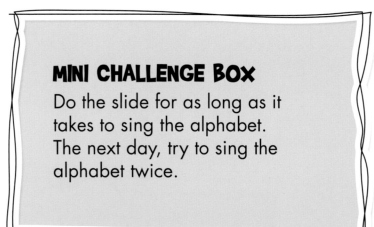

**MINI CHALLENGE BOX**
Do the slide for as long as it takes to sing the alphabet. The next day, try to sing the alphabet twice.

# Slow. . .fast

Going slowly, then going quickly, and then going slowly again, helps to increase your speed. This is called changing your **pace**.

**MINI CHALLENGE BOX**
Use a stopwatch to time yourself running up and down your street. Every other day, try it again. See if you can get faster each time.

Try jogging up and down your street, or on a running track. But add bursts of speed as you jog. For example, you could **sprint** from one lamp-post to the next, or around the bends of the track. Do slow jogs in between to catch your breath.

You can ask a friend to time you as you run.

# Knowing when to stop

Exercise is great for you. But there are times when you should take a break.

Stop exercising when your body needs a rest.

Here are three times when you should stop exercising:

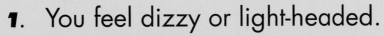

1.  You feel dizzy or light-headed.
2.  You feel sick.
3.  You hurt yourself (for example, if you twist your ankle). If you continue to exercise, you could make your injury worse.

 Take water breaks, too. You need to drink plenty of water when you exercise.

# Eating well

Eating well plays a big part in getting faster. Do you know the right things to eat? Try this quiz and find out!

1. How many servings of fruit and vegetables do you need each day?
   **A**. 0–2
   **B**. 3–5
   **C**. 6–10

2. True or false: It is fine to skip breakfast sometimes.

3. Two hours before exercise, you feel hungry. What is the best snack to eat?
   **A**. Ice cream
   **B**. Cheeseburger and chips
   **C**. An apple, some walnuts, and a muffin

You need to
eat lots of fruits
and vegetables
every day.

Healthy food can
be tasty, too.

# Big challenge

Football is a sport in which fast players rule. They use their bursts of speed to get to the ball first and race past defenders.

You could become a football star one day with lots of practice and speed training. It could be just the sport for you to show off your new speedy self!

One day you might be able to play for your favourite team.

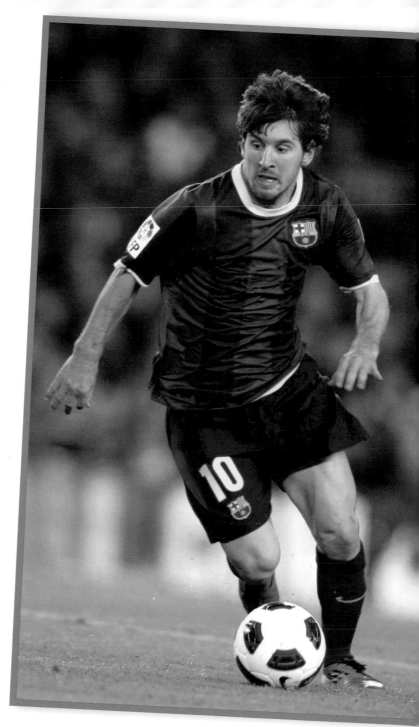

# Glossary

**coordination**  ability to get different parts of the body to work well together

**exaggerate**  to make something greater or more noticeable

**hydrated**  when a person has enough water in their body to stay healthy

**pace**  steady speed of walking or running

**sprint**  run very fast for a short distance

**stamina**  power to keep going or keep doing something

**strain**  to harm or injure

**stride**  long step

**sweat**  to release water through your skin

**warm up**  to do gentle exercise at the beginning of a workout. A warm up is used to get the body's muscles warm and loose.

# Find out more

## Books

*Athletics*, Rebecca Hunter (Franklin Watts, 2009)

*Football* (Sport and My Body), Charlotte Guillain (Raintree, 2010)

*Healthy Eating* (Health Choices), Cath Senker (Wayland, 2007)

## Websites

physicaleducationresources.com/warmups_small_games_physical_education_resources.aspx
Find out lots of ideas for games and warm ups.

www.bam.gov
A website devoted to fitness and health for children, including exercise, safety, and eating tips.

www.footy4kids.co.uk
This website has lots of games for you to play to help you improve your football skills.

# Index